Nature's *Healing* Walks

Discover what your
Soul is searching for

ANORA FIRE

Copyright © 2022 Anora Fire.

All rights reserved. No part of this book may be used or reproduced by any means, graphic, electronic, or mechanical, including photocopying, recording, taping or by any information storage retrieval system without the written permission of the author except in the case of brief quotations embodied in critical articles and reviews.

Balboa Press books may be ordered through booksellers or by contacting:

Balboa Press
A Division of Hay House
1663 Liberty Drive
Bloomington, IN 47403
www.balboapress.com.au
AU TFN: 1 800 844 925 (Toll Free inside Australia)
AU Local: 0283 107 086 (+61 2 8310 7086 from outside Australia)

Because of the dynamic nature of the Internet, any web addresses or links contained in this book may have changed since publication and may no longer be valid. The views expressed in this work are solely those of the author and do not necessarily reflect the views of the publisher, and the publisher hereby disclaims any responsibility for them.

Any people depicted in stock imagery provided by Getty Images are models, and such images are being used for illustrative purposes only.
Certain stock imagery © Getty Images.

Interior Image Credit: Anora Fire

ISBN: 978-1-9822-9331-4 (sc)
ISBN: 978-1-9822-9332-1 (e)

Print information available on the last page.

Balboa Press rev. date: 12/28/2021

Nature's Healing Walks

Let the light illuminate and guide your path.

Breathe in positivity, peace and calmness; it will extend your Light to manifest your desires.

Your curiosity is a flame – shine brightly
and see how you can grow.

Allow your inner beauty to find a way through; you are more determined than you are allowing yourself to be.

To see the path ahead clearly, remove your
fear and increase your belief.

To feel fear means Instinct has been forgotten. Leave fear behind, reach out for your Freedom.

Uncertainty is a mystery we just haven't solved yet.

A negative situation is always a positive in disguise.
Let the wilderness take your negativity away;
feel the renewed lightness around you.

Ignorance is only awareness in hiding,
which do you choose?

Your path ahead is natures doorway to freedom. Free your mind, sense it in your heart, practice it in your daily world.

Choose to release negativity and embrace
your innate spiritual power.

Do not fear the unknown; it is telling you what you need to know and do.

To ignore negativity is not a weakness; it allows self-empowerment in.

If you ask the question, be open to allowing the answer in.

Fear is not shameful; it is your challenge
to grow your heart and mind.

Wear your Light as your shield against negativity,
your fear will fade like the morning mist.

Do not feed your fear, it cannot exist when you say No.

Do not allow anxiety to feed your pain; let in the essence of nature to brighten your heart and Soul.

Draw on and breathe in Natures Energy, it is protecting you always even when you feel alone.

Focus on your reflection, it will bring you
the answers you are searching for.

Listen to the clouds, they sense your darkness yet are offering the Love you are searching for.

With ease the sun-light glides through the dark clouds; breathe in its energy and empower your soul. Each day is a new beginning if you choose it to be.

As the sun rises and gently fights the darkness, feel your Energy rise to make the choices you know are right.

The future you imagine is within your grasp.
Walk the path to where you want to be it may
not be as uncomfortable as it seems.

Step out of the shadows, everything you need is here.

Smile to yourself and be happy to be YOU.

REPEAT: I am safe, I am worthy, I am loved.

When the dawn comes, open your eyes to the sky and feel the Light it brings with it; it shows the pathway to what you need; will you follow it or remain in the shadows?

Do not ask 'How', Trust and you will know.

You have always been strong enough; trust yourself and you will make the right choices.

You are the Light on Your Life's journey, but also for those who travel with and behind you.

Be curious and you will find untold treasures
blossoming around you. Stand out, you
are meant to Shine and be heard.

If there is fear and confusion in your life, breathe in the serenity of nature, it will cleanse away the torment.

Take the time to discover the sense of 'no time, no place' and feel at one with the healing powers of the Universe.

A steady stream can become a powerful ocean; encourage yourself soak up that energy and radiate your resilience.

Immerse yourself in the energizing stillness. Silence has the power to challenge and awaken your dreams.

Complexity is an awakening beauty.

Struggling for direction, Trust, Believe and you will always find the right way through.

The quicker, shorter way may be easier.
Though the longer way to where you
are going is often the Truer way.

We have to try many choices before we arrive on the right path. How else do we know it's the right path?

When you're ready to stand out, you will.

When you know your way, it will be a smooth journey.

Shimmering reflections. Feel your heart
sing like the birds around you.

If it seems impossible, be determined, thrive and flourish. "I'm-possible" is what you really are.

When your light is determined to shine through, it will find a way to glow. Leave the darkness behind, it does not serve your True purpose.

Stand tall. Open your mind, and your heart will radiate its glowing energy for all to see.

In the hidden corners of your mind, you
will find a glimpse of the light waiting
to erupt into a furnace of life.

Believe in yourself, and like the floating mist, you will rise and rise to astounding heights.

In the stillness of your mind, you will find the answers when you listen.

Ground yourself to Earths vibrant energy and
allow colour to answer your worries.

Fear and confusion will hold you back from what you are meant to do; do what you are meant to do and fear and confusion will run away.

Look into your Soul and search through the pages of your memory, the answers were there all along.

Even if you hide your Light, it will find a way through.

Do not hide your truth, deal with the difficulties,
they will always return in uncertain ways if
you continue to deny your true feelings.

Your journey for Truth is within sight; what is the Truth you search for? Look into your eyes and it will be there.

When you tell yourself the truth and its uncomfortable, that's todays challenge

Immerse yourself in Nature and be at Home in the arms of the nurturing trees and cleansing waters.

Allowing Nature to guide your mind will show your heart the way to regain the Energy and Connection you crave.

Even in the confusion clarity will come when
you allow it a place by your side.

Focus, breathe, sink into yourself. Feel your heart expand and fill your Soul with love.

You still have the energy of fire in your Soul, use it to reach up to the stars that are waiting to applaud you.

When the time is right, your Guardian Angel
will show you your full potential.

126

About *the* Author

Anora Fire is an Energy Healer, Empath, Lightworker. She has a Bachelor of Health Nutritional Medicine, Bachelor of Nursing, Reiki Master. She inspires to Guide others into Nature to quieten the mind and re-discover their Spiritual connection to Self and Intuition.

CPSIA information can be obtained
at www.ICGtesting.com
Printed in the USA
LVRC080027240222
711888LV00004B/34